BISA, YOU ARE

Written by Martina M Lanier

Illustrated by Pallavi Kumari

Bisa, You Are.

Writers Kornered Publishing
The Healing Woman023 LLC
Text Copyright :copyright:2021 Martina Lanier
Illustrations Copyright :copyright:2021 : Pullavi Kumari
All rights reserved.

ISBN: 978-1-7372257-8-2

Books can be purchased in bulk by emailing WritersKornered@gmail.com

First Edition; Special Edition

Hi, I'm Bisa Mostafa, and today my baba and I are heading to the county fair for our daddy-daughter date. I am so excited.

On our way to the fair, Baba always lets me sit in the front seat. It makes me feel like a big girl and very special.

At the fair, there were so many people, so much to do, and I couldn't wait to do it all!
"Baba, I want to do everything," I yelled excitedly, jumping up and down.

"Baba, please can I go on the carousel? I love horses!"
"Of course, Bisa," Baba said as we got into the line.

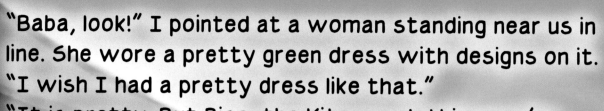

"Baba, look!" I pointed at a woman standing near us in line. She wore a pretty green dress with designs on it. "I wish I had a pretty dress like that."

"It is pretty. But Bisa, the Kitenge clothing you're wearing is just as beautiful." Baba smiled at me.

When it was my turn to get onto the carousel, Baba helped me get on the pretty pink horse. Pink is my favorite.

I had so much fun on the carousel that Baba and I went around one more time. As the carousel went around and around, I saw a girl with long hair. It was flying all around, and it looked awesome.

"Oh, Baba! I wish my hair was long like that." I pointed as we got off the carousel.

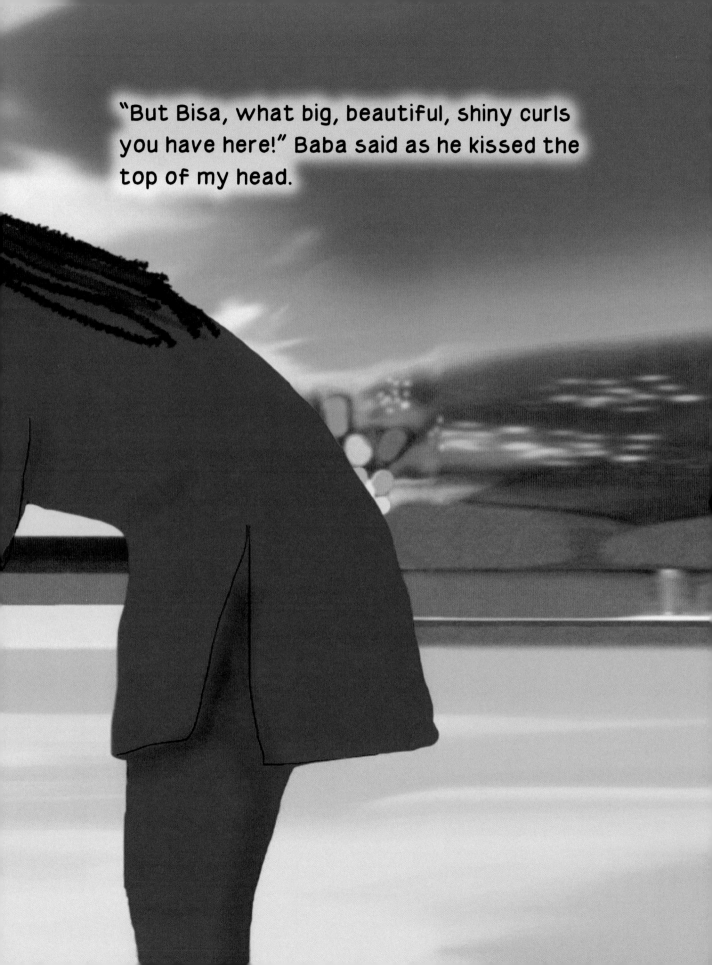

"But Bisa, what big, beautiful, shiny curls you have here!" Baba said as he kissed the top of my head.

Baba and I went onto the bumper cars. Then we got funnel cakes and hot dogs, so we sat down to eat. As I ate my funnel cake, I noticed the sun was shining so brightly, that Baba's eyes looked golden!

"Oh Baba, I wish I had golden eyes like you!"

"But Bisa, if you had golden eyes like me, who would have the big brown eyes that I love on you now?" Baba asked.

"But Baba, Mother has the same eyes as me!" I pouted.
"And I love seeing them on both of you every single day."
Baba smiled at me.

"Oh Baba, look! Can you please win me a bear?" I asked as we headed toward a ball-throwing game. "You're stronger than me, Baba. You'll hit all the bottles!"
"Oh Bisa, you are strong, and if you believe you can hit the bottles, you will. Come, let's try."

Baba gave money to the man, and we were both given
three bottles each.
"But Baba, I'm no good at this!" I whined as I missed
the first throw. "I wish I had long arms like you so that
I could be strong and hit the bottles!"

"Bisa, you are growing, and you are strong. Let's focus. Take a look at which set of bottles you would like to hit and zero in on it. Before throwing the ball, Bisa, know that you can do it. Ready?"

I nodded yes and zeroed in on the set of bottles I wanted to hit. "I know I can do this," I whispered over and over before throwing the ball.

"Bisa, you did it!" Baba yelled, picking me up and hugging me.

Baba's arms were full by the end of the night. I rode so many rides, played so many games, and won so many prizes that I was exhausted, so we headed home.

"Wow, Bisa! Did you win all of this?" Mother asked as she gave me a big hug.
"Baba too! We even won a big bear for you, Mother!"

"I'll be sure to keep this gift forever. How about we put all this up and get ready for bed?"

After my shower, Mother read me a bedtime story, and then I told her all about my day at the fair. I told her all about the beautiful dress I wanted and the long hair I wished I had. I told her how I wished I was as strong as Baba and had his golden eyes.

Mother smiled at me, rubbing my face. "Do you know what your name means, Bisa?"
"No, Mother. Please tell me!" I asked with wide eyes.

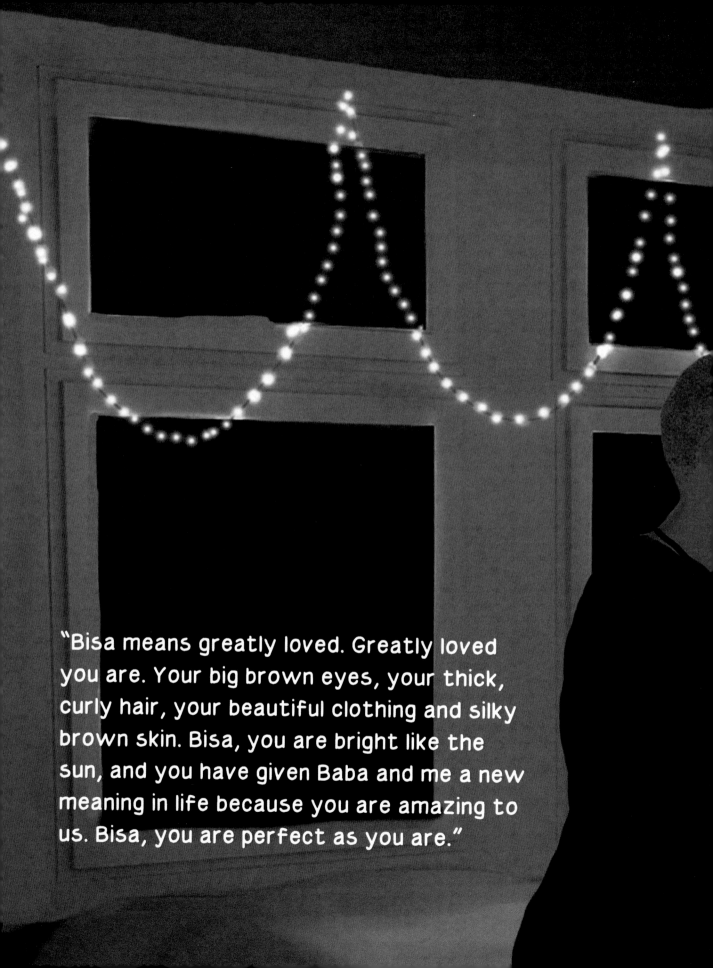

"Bisa means greatly loved. Greatly loved you are. Your big brown eyes, your thick, curly hair, your beautiful clothing and silky brown skin. Bisa, you are bright like the sun, and you have given Baba and me a new meaning in life because you are amazing to us. Bisa, you are perfect as you are."

"But Mother, sometimes I just want to be different."
"Bisa, you are different, and that's what makes
you the most special girl in the world. And don't you
forget that." Mother kissed me on the forehead
before turning my night-light on and leaving my room.
"Goodnight, my beautiful Bisa."

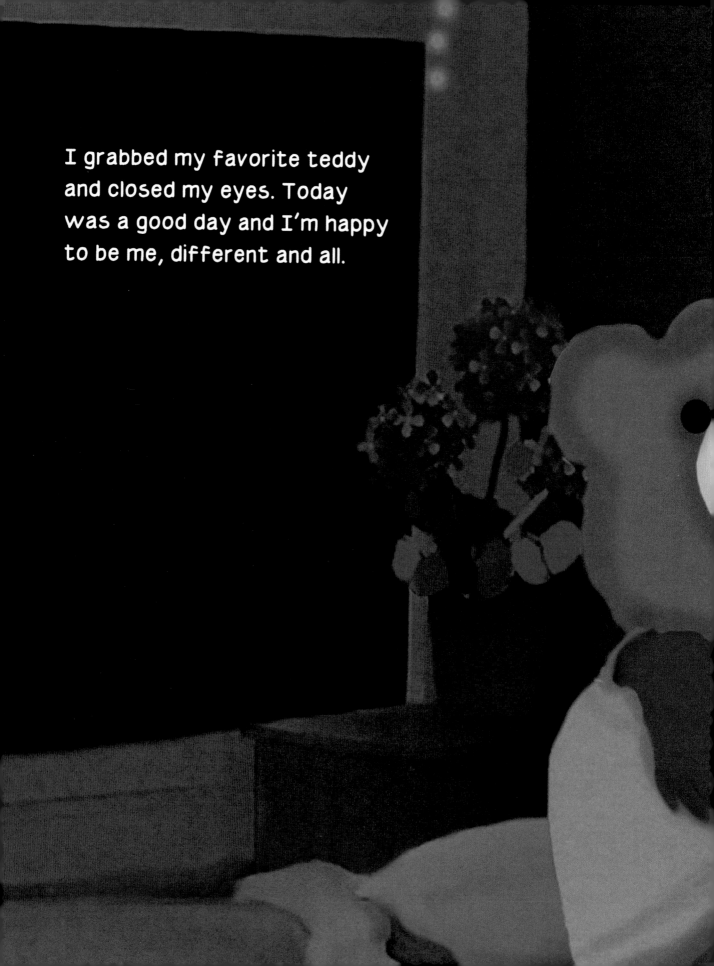

I grabbed my favorite teddy and closed my eyes. Today was a good day and I'm happy to be me, different and all.

Made in the USA
Middletown, DE
10 October 2021